U.S. GOVERNMENT IN REVIEW

# WHY WE VOTE

BY KATHRYN WALTON

Enslow PUBLISHING

Please visit our website, www.enslow.com. For a free color catalog of all our high-quality books, call toll free 1-800-398-2504 or fax 1-877-980-4454.

**Library of Congress Cataloging-in-Publication Data**
Names: Walton, Kathryn, 1993- author.
Title: Why we vote / Kathryn Walton.
Description: Buffalo, NY : Enslow Publishing, 2025. | Series: U.S. government in review | Includes bibliographical references and index.
Identifiers: LCCN 2023042318 | ISBN 9781978538207 (library binding) | ISBN 9781978538191 (paperback) | ISBN 9781978538214 (ebook)
Subjects: LCSH: Voting–United States–Juvenile literature. | Elections–United States–Juvenile literature.
Classification: LCC JK1978 .W354 2025 | DDC 324.60973–dc23/eng/20230915
LC record available at https://lccn.loc.gov/2023042318

Published in 2025 by
**Enslow Publishing**
2544 Clinton Street
Buffalo, NY 14224



Portions of this work were originally authored by Santana Hunt and published as *Why Do We Vote?* All new material in this edition is authored by Kathryn Walton.

Designer: Leslie Taylor
Editor: Natalie Humphrey

Photo credits: Cover (photo) Moab Republic/Shutterstock.com; series art (background) Apostrophe/Shutterstock.com; p. 5 vesperstock/Shutterstock.com; p.7 Lucky-photographer/Shutterstock.com; p.8 Rosamar/Shutterstock.com; p. 9 chrisdorney/Shutterstock.com; p. 10 Andrey_Popov/Shutterstock.com; p. 11 AR30MM Ariel Ruff/Shutterstock.com; p. 13 Trong Nguyen/Shutterstock.com; p. 14 Trevor Bexon/Shutterstock.com; p. 15 lev radin/Shutterstock.com; p. 16 lev radin/Shutterstock.com; pp. 19, 21 Rob Crandall/Shutterstock.com; p. 20 WESTOCK PRODUCTIONS/Shutterstock.com; p. 23 Everett Collection/iStock.com; p.24 Harmony Video Production/Shutterstock.com; p. 25 PF-(usna)/Alamy.com; p. 27 Allison C Bailey/Shutterstock.com; p. 29 vesperstock/iStockphoto.com.



Printed in the United States of America

Some of the images in this book illustrate individuals who are models. The depictions do not imply actual situations or events.

CPSIA compliance information: Batch #CSENS25: For further information, contact Enslow Publishing at 1-800-398-2504.

# CONTENTS



*Words in the glossary appear in **bold** the first time they are used in the text.*

# Voting in the United States

Voting is the way every U.S. citizen gets a say in their government. In the past, the **Founding Fathers** let states decide who could vote, and many states had narrow rules about voting. Voting today looks different than during the first U.S. **elections**, but it is still just as important!

## LEARN MORE

The states only gave white men who owned land the right to vote in the 1700s, when the United States was founded. Today, any U.S. **citizen** over the age of 18 has the right to vote!

# The Republic

In the United States, citizens vote for people to **represent** them in the government. This type of government is called a republic. In the United States, elected representatives serve in Congress. Congress is made up of two houses: the Senate and the House of Representatives.

In the United States, people vote for national government leaders, such as members of Congress, and local government leaders, like mayors and city council members.

## LEARN MORE

U.S. Capitol Building, where Congress meets

# Elections

In the United States, there are two main times when people vote in elections. In a primary, a candidate is chosen from many candidates trying to represent a certain political party in the general election. A candidate is a person running for a government office.

## LEARN MORE

A political party is a group of people who share beliefs about how the government should be run.

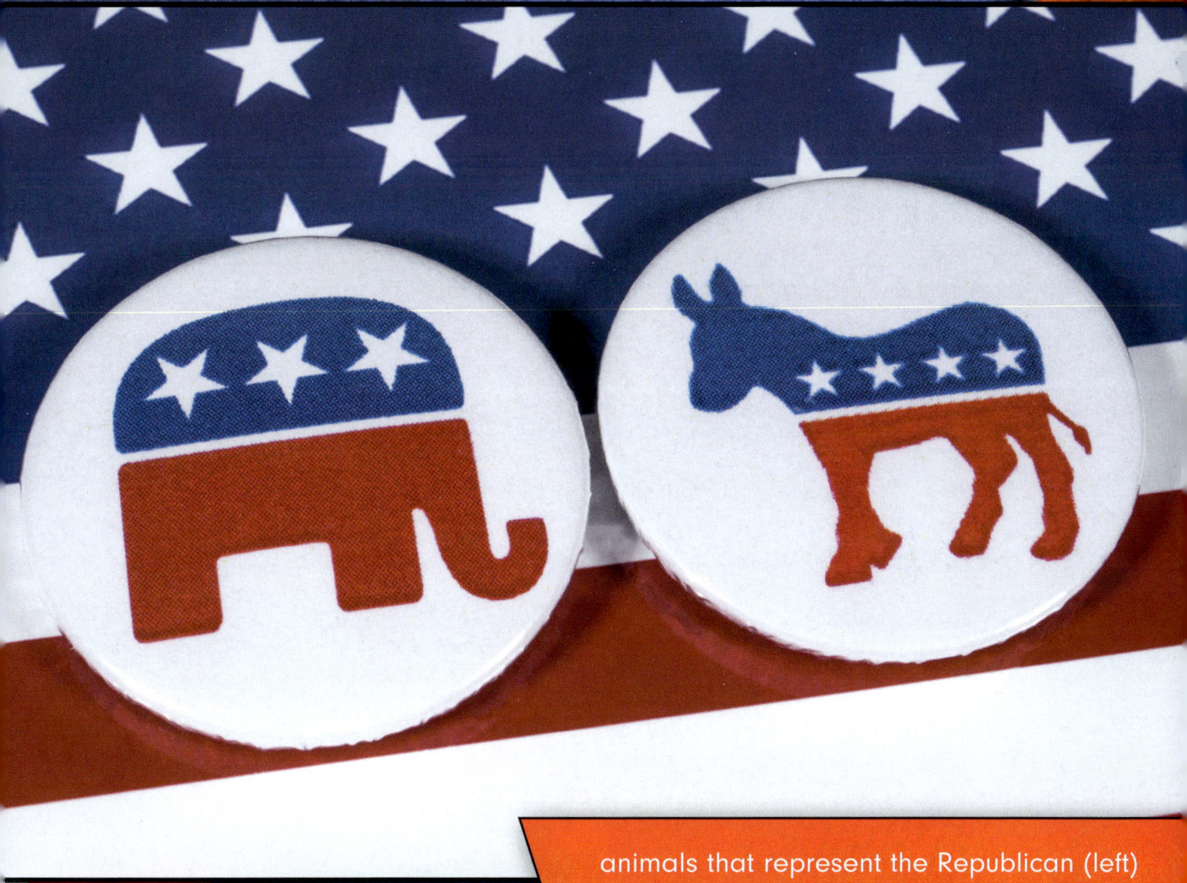

animals that represent the Republican (left) and Democratic political parties

After the primary election comes the general election. Voters in a general election can choose from the winners of the primaries. The winner of a general election then takes on the position they were running for, such as mayor. In general elections, voters can vote for any candidate.

## LEARN MORE

During a closed primary election, voters can only vote for candidates within their political party.

# Knowing the Candidates

In any election, it's important for voters to know what the candidates stand for. Voters are choosing who will represent them in the local, state, and **federal** government. These choices can affect the daily lives of you and everyone you know!

## LEARN MORE

In some state and local elections, voters can also vote on propositions. Propositions are **proposals** for new state and local laws.

Voters choose who will run schools, cities, and police departments in local elections. They also vote for who will oversee a town's budget, among other jobs. In a congressional election, voters decide who will represent their state in the federal government.

## LEARN MORE

Elected **officials** serve a certain amount of time in office. This is called a term. Many officials are allowed to serve more than one term.

Congressman Hakeem Jeffries

# The Popular Vote

Many elections in the United States are decided by a popular vote. The popular vote is the total number of votes people cast in an election. The elections for U.S. president and vice president are decided by the Electoral College instead of the popular vote.

President Joe Biden

The Electoral College is the process by which a group of people called electors vote for a certain candidate. When citizens cast their vote for the president, they're voting for electors who have promised to vote for that candidate!

LEARN MORE

# How Many People Vote?

Even though millions of U.S. citizens can vote, many don't! In fact, many elections see less than half of the **eligible** voters at the polls. Voter turnout, or how many people show up to vote, can greatly change who ends up in office.

## LEARN MORE

The 2020 election had the highest voter turnout in the 2000s. Even then, only about 66.8 percent of citizens over 18 voted!

There are many reasons voters may not show up to vote. Some may not be registered, or signed up, to vote. Some voters don't have enough time to vote. In states like Mississippi, citizens must register to vote by 30 days before the election!

## LEARN MORE

In some states, people charged with a crime cannot vote while they're in **prison**.

# Voter Rights

Under the original U.S. Constitution, not everyone had the right to vote. Women and non-white citizens were refused the right to vote. Throughout history, many people worked to pass amendments to change the **Constitution** and give these groups the rights they deserved.

**LEARN MORE**

An amendment is a change to the Constitution. The Fifteenth Amendment gave non-white men the right to vote. The Nineteenth Amendment gave women the right to vote.

The Voting Rights Act was passed in 1965 to stop voter **discrimination**. It made it illegal to stop someone from voting because of their race. It also made testing any voters before they voted illegal. Even today, voter discrimination still happens though.

## LEARN MORE

The Voting Rights Act may not have gotten rid of discrimination altogether, but it did help to raise voter turnout.

President Lyndon B. Johnson signing the Voting Rights Act

# Creating Change

When people vote, they aren't just choosing leaders, they are causing change! If voters aren't happy with what the government is doing, they can use their vote to speak up. Voters can choose someone new for a government position who can change what the government is doing.

**LEARN MORE**

While it's uncommon for a single vote to change an election, a group of people voting together can make a difference.

# Voting Today

Some people want to change voting in the United States. Many want the president to be chosen by a popular vote. Others think people should always be able to vote, even if they're in jail. With the right to vote, a person's voice can be heard in their government.

## LEARN MORE

For many people, voting is an important part of the political, or government, process! They believe it's their duty as U.S. citizens to vote.

# Landmark Voting Rights Amendments

**1870**

## FIFTEENTH AMENDMENT

The Fifteenth Amendment gives African American men the right to vote.

**1920**

## NINETEENTH AMENDMENT

The Nineteenth Amendment gives women the right to vote.

**1964**

## TWENTY-FOURTH AMENDMENT

The Twenty-Fourth Amendment removes taxes at the polls.

**1971**

## TWENTY-SIXTH AMENDMENT

The Twenty-Sixth Amendment lowers the voting age from 21 to 18.

# GLOSSARY

**citizen:** Someone who lives in a country legally and has certain rights.

**constitution:** The basic laws by which a country or state is governed.

**discrimination:** Unfairly treating people unequally because of their race or beliefs.

**election:** The act of voting someone into a government position.

**eligible:** Being qualified to do something.

**federal:** Having to do with the national government.

**Founding Father:** A leader in the founding of the United States of America.

**official:** A person in a position of authority.

**prison:** A place of captivity, commonly for those who break the law.

**proposal:** Something, such as a suggestion or plan, that is presented for a group of people's consideration.

**represent:** To stand for.

# For More Information

## Books

Lombardo, Jennifer. *What Are Voting Rights?* Buffalo, NY: KidHaven Publishing, 2022.

Normandeau, Sheryl. *Fair Elections and Voting Rights.* San Diego, CA: BrightPoint, 2024.

## Website

**We Want to Vote: Battles for the Ballot**
*kids.nationalgeographic.com/history/article/we-want-to-vote-battles-for-the-ballot*
Find out more about the people who fought for the right to vote and the amendments created because of them.

***Publisher's note to educators and parents:*** *Our editors have carefully reviewed this website to ensure that it is suitable for students. Many websites change frequently, however, and we cannot guarantee that a site's future contents will continue to meet our high standards of quality and educational value. Be advised that students should be closely supervised whenever they access the internet.*

# Index